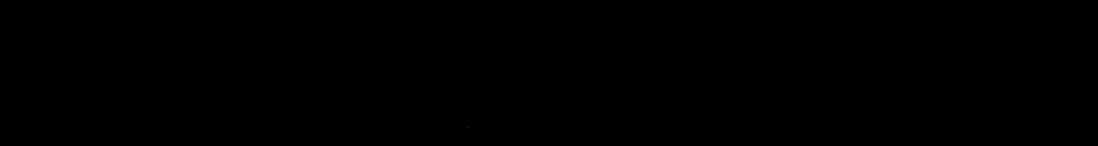

Along the Cowboy Trail

The quiet solitude of the pristine wilderness west of the Mississippi was suddenly broken by the thunderous roar of a new industry, and millions of hooves now pounded the once-undisturbed prairies. In the choking dust of a sudden rush to conquer the forbidden frontier, a hero emerged — a new breed of man, with a will forged of steel and a heart set on adventure. Nearly as wild as the land he sought to tame, he was kin to the harsh elements he battled — fire, wind and flood; kin to the meanest beasts — the coyote, the mountain lion and the rattlesnake. He was blood and guts and nerves and heart, and he came to be known as the cowboy. ~

The American Cowboy in Photographs, Verse, and Lore
~Photography by Robert Dawson ~Text and editing by Tammy LeRoy

*This book is
dedicated to the men and horses
who came before.* ~

Publishied by RD Publishing Inc
PO Box 44121
Phoenix, AZ 85064
(480) 483-5336
Website: dawsonphotography.com
Email: mail@dawsonphotography.com

Photography - Robert Dawson
Text & Editing - Tammy LeRoy

Design, Production, Print- Mark Kashino
KEI - Kashino Enterprises Inc
Website: kashino.com
Email: mark@kashino.com

Second Printing
Printed in Korea

Library of Congress Control Number
00-091184

ISBN 0-9678881-0-7

The cowboys photographed for this book, who gave their time and their talents, are dedicated to preserving the cowboy's way of life in the West. Others helped with livestock and equipment, and all were dedicated to producing the best photographs possible. Many who helped out are dear friends. Without them, this book would not have become a reality. A heartfelt thanks to all: Robert Dawson, Sr., Charles Motley, Wayne Ramey, Cody McGuire, Billy A. Stewart, Matt Motley, Lance Weaver, June Connacher, Dan Turcotte, Donna Eddings, Tim Dawson, Wes Walton, Luke Walton, and all the hands at the Lone Tree Bible Ranch in Glendo, Wyo., Gino and Angela D'Ambrose, Rolf Flake, Bobbie Deschenes, Brett Deschenes, Broc Deschenes, Jerry Zollinger, Wade Zollinger, Tony Jardine, Toby Lapp, Jerry and Kathy Tarantino, Greg Worley, Larry Brady and Roger Sabori.

A special thanks to those who were so supportive during the writing of this book. Thier input and constant encouragement made this project possible: Rene Kuehne, Phil and Stephanie Farber, Ron and Carolyn McConkey, Bob and Terry Hutt, Brandi Hazen, James Hellwig, Jessica Hellwig, Wally Taylor, Kathy Khoury, Peter Aleshire and Marshall Trimble. Without your love and support, this book could not have been written. Mark Kashino, of Kashino Design, is also appreciated for his talent in the lay-out and design of this book.

A million thanks to you all,

May God bless and keep you. May your saddle stay dry and your horse never stumble. May you ride in the wind's direction. May you live a cowboy's dream.

Tammy LeRoy, Editor

P R E F A C E

This book was created to give a poignant glimpse of the American cowboy through the camera lens and through written reflections on the cowboy life. Robert Dawson's eye for idyllic locations, and his ability to create a distinct ambiance, are the foundations for its design. Idealistic and sentimental by design, this book does not give an all-inclusive representation of the cowboy, especially the cowboy in the present day.

It is not the intent of the author or the photographer to render a comprehensive look at all of the idiosyncrasies and accouterments associated with cowboys. Nor is it our goal to educate the reader in depth on the complex history or the present circumstances of the ranching industry.

The photographs and selections of verse used in this book are romantic representations of the cowboy's life. Many ideas and institutions associated with true cowboys are barely touched on in these pages — Mexican vaqueros, Western justice, saloons, ladies of the night, gunfights, and rodeos, to name a few.

Cowboy poems and songs cover a multitude of topics, but verse was selected here to emphasize the mood of the photographs, and of the book as a whole. Excerpts of texts were chosen with the same criteria, and short essays were added to give a better understanding of cowboy life. Many of the verses recount common situations in a cowboy's life or lament the inevitable passing of the cowboy lifestyle and the disappearing of the open range.

Many of the selections that were chosen are cherished classics, written by some of the most respected cowboy poets. Others are traditional rhymes by unknown authors and have been changed or added to throughout the years. Some are contemporary works crafted by those who still live the cowboy life in the western states. Those not familiar with cowboy terms may find that reading the lexicon will add clarity to many of the selections.

Verse was used to enhance, but not to draw attention away from the photographs or to compromise the pages aesthetically, and most of the poems were not printed in their entirety. A conscientious effort was made to give proper credit to authors. It is our hope that this book will stand as a tribute to the cowboy as an enduring symbol of the American West. ~

INTRODUCTION

Robert Dawson's outstanding photographs stir within us a nostalgic yearning for an America that once was — a wide-open expanse of untamed wilderness; a big land, where the biggest of dreams could come true. No group has stood as a symbol of our cherished frontier more than the American cowboy. He is an icon, representing the values that make Americans unique: courage and self-reliance, dogged determination and unbridled spirit.

Dawson's photographs capture both the essence of the cowboy and the grandeur of the West. Scouting for locations on horseback, he has a knack for finding ideal settings, matchless scenery and perfect lighting. The photographs, taken in Arizona, Idaho, Montana, New Mexico and Wyoming, seem to embody the spirit and the romance of the old frontier.

Those of us who have been acquainted with working cowboys know his idealistic image is not entirely fictional. The attributes bestowed on him in print and film, such as courage, wisdom and chivalry, are more true-to-life than many might expect.

In truth, cowboys make up a unique subculture. Nostalgic by nature, they relish their connection with the past. Most have a higher appreciation for good, common sense than for education, and the values they hold tend to be on the old-fashioned side. Though one may find a cowboy engaged in activities that would be frowned upon by moralists, his culture has a strict code of ethics of its own. Arizona cowboy, Doug Moock, says the values are simple: "Try to live the life you believe in every day. Be a good man, a good husband, a good dad, a top hand. Never leave a man in a bind."

Though they may display an outward humility, most cowboys consider themselves a cut above the ordinary man, if not by natural endowment, then by good fortune. Cowboys love spending time in the big outdoors. Few would give up the long hours and dangerous work for an easier, better-paying job in the city.

The songs and poems included in this book are a part of a long-standing tradition. Since the beginning of cattle ranching on the frontier, poetry has been as much a time-honored part of a cowpuncher's life as spring and fall roundups. It may not fit our rugged image of the lone drifter on horseback, but cowboys have always been poets.

~ 4

Continued on page 8

The men who were first hired on to do the work of the cowboy came from various occupations. Some knew the works of Kipling, Shakespeare and Wordsworth, and were familiar with Irish and English ballads. Making up poems was a way to occupy the time alone and to pass on stories. Verse was often put to a tune to lull cattle and to break up the monotony.

On the trail, a cowboy's work lasted from sun-up to sundown, but he was seldom in a hurry because cattle need to be moved at a leisurely pace. There was a lot of time alone to appreciate the environment and to reflect on what he had seen throughout his life.

Many cowboy poems are rhyming tales of life on the range, greatly embellished and often humorous. Much of the verse laments the disappearing cowboy lifestyle and Old West code of honor. A joke that circulates around the cowboy poetry gatherings asks, "How many cowboys does it take to change a light bulb?" The answer is two: One to put in the new bulb, and another to write a poem about how much he misses the old one.

The myth surrounding the cowboy is a mix of fantasy and reality. He captures our imaginations and our hearts. Arizona historian, Marshall Trimble, describes his importance to American culture:[1]

> *The cowboy riding atop his trusty steed is America's answer to the knights of old. These heroic figures have come to symbolize all the manifestations of character we ascribe to winning the West. Their grand image represents the highest and most honorable qualities of mankind: the outdoors, freedom, individualism and defense of the oppressed. The cowboy seems so indigenous to our culture that, had he never existed, we would have invented him.*

The American cowboy is disappearing as rapidly as the open range grazing lands that made his existence both possible and necessary. Reluctantly, we let him pass, but his legacy will remain. ~

[1] *Arizona: A Cavalcade of history, by Marshall Trimble. Treasure Chest Publications, Tucson, Arizona 1989.*

Previous pages: Four Peaks, Arizona

Before the storm. Pariah Plateau, Arizona

Along the Cowboy Trail

Along the dusty trail they ride,
These cowboys with their dreams.
Their homes are in their saddles
And they know what freedom means.

They spend their years on open range,
Their work is on the line.
Their job is done
When light is gone
And the cook calls dinner time.

Their time upon this earth is short
And their deeds are often sung
In rhyme of how the law is dealt
Through the barrel of a gun.

Some come to be our heroes,
While others land in jail.
But the legends grow
As their stories are told
Along the cowboy trail.

Robert Dawson
Phoenix, Arizona

Wyoming thunderstorm rolling in.

The Broncho Buster

I've busted bronchos off and on ever since I struck the trail,
I have saddled bronchos from nostril down to tail,
But I struck one down on Powder River, and Stranger,
    I'll be cussed,
'Twas the only living broncho that your servant couldn't bust.

When I got on he went so high that the lights from Zion shone.
Right there we parted company an' he come down alone.
When I at last struck turf again the broncho he was free;
I brought along a bunch of stars to dance in front of me.

I've sold my chaps and saddle, my spurs can lay and rust,
For once in a while there is a bronk that the devil himself
    can't bust.

Excerpted from:
Robert W. Gordon Collection - Library of Congress
Gordon 2351: manuscript

First day of school.

Our Little Cowgirl

(Traditional western ballad)

Thar she goes a-lopin', stranger,
Khaki-gowned, with flyin' hair,
Talk about your classy ridin'.—
Wal, you're gettin' it right thar.
Jest a kid, but lemme tell you
When she warms a saddle seat
On that outlaw bronc a-straddle
She is one that can't be beat!

Ride? Why she can cut a critter
From the herd as neat as pie,
Read a brand out on the ranges
Just as well as you or I.
Ain't much yet with the riata,
But you give her a few years
And no puncher with the outfit
Will beat her a-ropin' steers.

Proud o' her? Say, lemme tell you.
She's the queen of all the range;
Got a grip upon our heart-strings
Mighty strong, but that ain't strange;
'Cause she loves the lowin' cattle,
Loves the hills and open air.
Dusty trails on blossomed canons
God has strung around out here.

*Songs of the Cattle Trail
and the Cow Camp (82-83)
Quoted by John A. Lomax*

A Cowboy's Prayer

Oh Lord, I've never lived where churches grow,
  I loved creation better as it stood
That day you finished it so long ago
  And looked upon your work and called it good.
I know that others find you in the light
  That's sifted down through tinted window panes,
And yet I seem to feel you near tonight
  In the dim, quiet starlight on the plains.
I thank you Lord, that I am placed so well,
  That You have made my freedom so complete;
That I'm no slave of whistle, clock or bell,
Just let me live my life as I've begun
  And give me work that's open to the sky;
Make me a pardner of the wind and sun,
  And I won't ask for a life that's soft or high.

Excerpted from:
Badger Clark, Sun and Saddle Leather
Chapman and Grimes,
Boston, Mass. 1936

Peaceful reflections

"**I wish I could find words** to express the trueness, the bravery, the hardihood, the sense of honor, the loyalty to their trust and to each other of the old trail hands. They kept their places around a herd of cattle under all circumstances, and if they had to fight they were always ready. Timid men were not among them – the life did not fit them. . . . Despite all that has been said of him, the old-time cowboy is the most misunderstood man on earth. May the flowers prosper on his grave and ever bloom, for I can only salute him — in silence.

J. Evetts Haley, Charles Goodnight,
Cowman and Plainsman,
Houghton Mifflin Company, 1936

Grand Tetons, Wyoming

19 ~

"**So it is true** that you may enclose the green prairies and plow up the sweet wildflowers, you may build towns and cities on sites once occupied by the cowboy's dugout and branding pen, but always something of the fragrance of the romance of the early days will cling to the region which the bold range riders once called their own, to remind us of those picturesque days gone forever."

"The Romance of the Range"
West Texas Historical Year Book
Vol. V (June, 1929), 21

Sunrise in the Sierra Nevadas

" . . . **he swears like a trooper,** drinks like a fish, wears clothes like an actor, and fights like a devil. He is gracious to ladies, reserved toward strangers, generous to his friends, and brutal to his enemies. He is a cowboy, a typical Westerner."

Walter Prescott Webb
The Great Plains
Boston, Ginn and Company, 1931

Sawtooth Mountains, Idaho

A line camp visitor in Arizona

Separate trails.

The birth of the American cowboy came soon after the Civil War with the rapid settlement of the western territories. A range cattle industry became possible with the opening of the frontier, where more than a million square miles of uninhabited prairie was available for grazing livestock. The industry soon flourished in the West, and cattle became king.

Cowboys were laborers hired to drive herds on the famed cattle trails from the open range to market centers. Most cattle towns, such as Dodge City in Kansas, were near the western-most railroads of the time. In the heyday of the industry, some historians estimate that as many as six million head of cattle and 40,000 cowboys were in the West. The average drive employed ten cowboys for about a dollar a day each, and 2,500 to 3,000 cows were moved.

The cattle were moved slowly and allowed to graze along the way. Driving a herd too fast meant lost weight, which was the equivalent of lost profits. Most herds were trailed an average of ten miles per day and driving a herd to market often took two to three months. The trail boss usually rode in front of the group while other hands flagged the herd in different positions. The camp cook, who often served as doctor and barber, drove a chuckwagon in which all supplies for the outfit were hauled.

Previous pages: Grand Tetons, Wyoming.

Continued on next page.

Well-broke cowponies were essential to the cowboy's job. The remuda, or string of horses used by the outfit, could be as large as forty head. The cowboy who took care of the remuda was called a wrangler. Horses were worked hard and a cowboy usually changed mounts several times a day. The best mounts were reserved for the important job of riding night herd. Contrary to myth, few cowboys owned their own horses.

The bravery of these cowboys is one characteristic that has not been exaggerated in movies and folklore. There were many dangers along the trail, and lives were often lost. Falls, stampedes, and attacks by Indians or outlaws could have grave consequences. Most cowboys were very loyal to the brand they rode for, sometimes risking their lives to protect the cattle. Those who hired on as cowboys came from various places, for various reasons. Many came from southern states, hoping to leave the war-torn South as far behind them as possible. Some were educated men from England or Scotland, looking for adventure. Blacks, Mexicans and Indians made up a good part of the cowboy population.

For the most part, the job was considered to be menial labor, and the majority of cowboys were in their teens or early twenties. It was difficult work. A day on the trail lasted fourteen hours, usually followed by a two-hour shift of night guard. The scorching sun and the suffocating dust stirred up by the herd were relentless tormentors.

The days of the great cattle drives — immortalized in print and motion pictures — only lasted from about 1867 to 1890. The introduction of a railroad system further west made the long drives to market unnecessary, and the majority of cowboy work became ranch work.

Ranches sprang up in the West wherever there was water. A rancher generally claimed any land within ten or twenty miles of a watering source. These claims were enforced by federal laws and, when necessary, with a loaded rifle. The invention of the barbed wire fence further guaranteed land claims.

Continued on next page.

Bringing in the rogue. Lone Pine, California

From the mid-1870s to the mid-1880s, large and small outfits sharing the same vast grazing area would hold collaborative roundups in the fall and spring. The cattle belonging to each brand were doctored, branded, castrated, de-horned and separated for market at roundup. A dozen brands and several thousand head of cattle were often involved in these mammoth events. Although roundups today are not nearly as large, the cowboy's work at roundup remains largely the same.

Today, for the most part, only large outfits are able to survive economically. Grazing regulations and rivalry for land use from developers and environmentalists have greatly reduced herd sizes. But the demand for beef allows the cattlegrowing industry to continue, and as long as there is a cattle industry, the working cowboy will remain an ongoing fixture in the West. ~

Early morning ride in northern Arizona.

The Cowboy

Oh, a man there lives on the western plains,
With a ton of fight and an ounce of brains,
Who herds the cows as he robs the trains
And goes by the name of cowboy.

He laughs at death and scoffs at life;
He feels unwell unless in some strife.
He fights with a pistol, a rifle, or knife,
This reckless, rollicking cowboy.

He sets up drinks when he hasn't a cent;
He'll fight like hell with any young gent.
When he makes love, he goes it hell-bent,
Oh, he's some lover, this cowboy.

He shoots out lights in a dancing hall;
He gets shot up in a drunken brawl.
Some coroner's jury then ends it all,
And that's the last of the cowboy.

Cowboy Sings
edited by Kenneth Clark
New York: Paull-Pioneer Music

. . . **It was a land of scattered ranches**, of herds of long-horned cattle, and of reckless riders who unmoved looked in the eyes of life or of death. In that land we led a free and hardy life, with horse and with rifle. We worked under the scorching midsummer sun, when the wide plains simmered and wavered in the heat; and we knew the freezing misery of riding night guard around the cattle in the late fall round-up. In the soft springtime the stars were glorious in our eyes each night before we fell asleep; and in the winter we rode through blinding blizzards, when the driven snow-dust burnt our faces. There were monotonous days, as we guided the trail cattle or the beef herds, hour after hour, at the slowest of walks; and minutes or hours teeming with excitement as we stopped stampedes or swam the herds across rivers treacherous with quicksands or brimmed with running ice. We knew toil and hardship and hunger and thirst; and we saw men die violent deaths as they worked among the horses and cattle, or fought in evil feuds with one another; but we felt the beat of hardy life in our veins, and ours was the glory of work and the joy of living.

From Theodore Roosevelt, An Autobiography, pp. 93-94.
Copyright, 1913, by Charles Scribner's Sons;
1941, by Edith Carow Roosevelt.
New York: Charles Scribner's sons.

The Old Cowboy

I rode a line on the open range,
When cow-punching wasn't slow;
I've turned a longhorn cow one way,
And the other the buffalo.

I've stood night guard many a night
In the face of a driving storm,
And sang to them a doleful song
when they rattled their hocks and horns.

They're building towns and railroads now,
Where we used to bed our cows;
And the man with the mule, the plow and the hoe
Is digging up our old bed grounds.

The old cowboy has watched the change,
Has seen the good times come and go—
But the old cowboy will soon be gone,
Just like the buffalo.

Excerpted from a song sung to Frank J. Dobie
by Charlie Johnson of Charco, Texas.
Dobie article, "More Ballads and Songs of the Frontier Folk"
Texas Folklore Society publication, Vol. VII, p.136.

Cowboys on the Pariah River.

Git Along, Cayuse

Arizona! the tramp of cattle.
  The biting dust and the raw red brand,
Shuffling sheep and the smoke of battle,
  The upturned face and the empty hand.

I was top hand once for the T-bar-T
  In the days of long ago.
But I took to seein' the scenery
  Where the barbed wire fence don't know.

I was top hand once, with the trail for mine
  And plenty of room to roam.
So now I'm riding the old chuck line
  And any old place is home.

Excerpted from: Hendren 5: manuscript.
(From the collection of
Stella M. Hendren of Kooskia, Idaho.)
Some stanzas have been traced to poems
by Henry Herbert Knibbs

Pariah Plateau, Arizona

Flying diamonds.

The Gal I Left Behind Me

I struck the trail in seventy-nine,
The herd strung out behind me;
As I jogged along my mind ran back
To the gal I left behind me.

If ever I get off the trail
And the Indians, they don't find me,
I'll make my way straight back again
To the gal I left behind me.

When the night was dark and the cattle run,
With the boys coming on behind me,
My mind run back at my pistol's crack
To the gal I left behind me.

The wind did blow, the rain did flow,
the hail did fall and blind me;
I thought of the gal, the sweet little gal,
The gal I left behind me.

*From Cowboy Songs
and Other Frontier Ballads
Collected by John A. Lomax
and Alan Lomax*

Children of the Trails

We have gathered
The wild children of the trails,
Burrs in their forelocks,
Sagebrush in their tails.

Horses with heart
Forged on rock and clay,
Raised on bark and brush,
Strangers to baled hay.

We sing a chant to draw them in,
To let them have some hope;
They'll never fear a saddle
Or be frightened of the rope.

A tune to gain their trust
And calm their shaking hides,
To make a willing mount
That will be some cowboy's pride.

Charles Motley
Payson, Arizona

Spring roundup on the Zollinger Ranch, Idaho

The Cowboy's Ride

Oh, for a ride o'er the prairies free,
  On a fiery untamed steed,
Where the curlews fly and the coyotes cry
And the western wind goes sweeping by,
  For my heart enjoys the speed.

With my left hand light on the bridle rein,
  And saddle girth pinched behind,
With a lariat tied at the pony's side
By my stout right arm that's true and tried,
  We race with the whistling wind.

We're up and away in the morning light
  As swift as a shooting star,
That suddenly flies across the sky,
And the wild birds whirl in quick surprise
  At the cowboy's gay "Hurrah!"

As free as a bird o'er the rolling sea
  We skim the pasture wide,
Like a seagull strong we hurry along,
And the earth resounds with a galloping song
  As we sail through the fragrant tide.

You can have your ride in the crowded town!
  Give me the prairies free.
Where the curlews fly and the coyotes cry,
And the heart expands 'neath the open sky:
  Oh, that's the ride for me!

Recorded by John A Lomax
Melody and Text: Library of Congress # 1338Ai

Cave Creek, Arizona

Grand Tetons, Wyoming

Freedom.

Chopo

Through rocky arroyos so dark and so deep,
Down the sides of the mountains so slippery and steep,
You've good judgment, sure footed, wherever you go,
You're a safety conveyance my little Chopo.

Whether single or double or in the lead of a team,
Over highways or byways or crossing a stream,
You're always in fix and willing to go
Whenever you're called on, my chico, Chopo.

You're a good roping horse, you were never jerked down..
When tied to steer, you will circle him round
Let him once cross the string, and over he'll go,
You *sabe* the business, my cow horse Chopo.

One day on the Llano, a hail storm began.
The herds were stampeded, the horses all ran.
The lightning it glittered, a cyclone did blow,
But you faced the sweet music my little Chopo.

Excerpted from:
Jack Thorp, News Print Shop
Estancia, New Mex. 1908

Arizona Cowboy

Giant Saguaro cactus, Arizona

~ 56

On the Trail From a Puncher's Point of View

You follow up the cattle for many a dreary mile,
The wind a constant blowing and the dust as thick as 'ile,
A steady churn of alkali that fills your eyes and nose,
And perhaps a sullin' dogie to round up your other woes.

You're spitting dimes from dryness, your tobacco don't taste right,
You strain your eyes to bursting but no water hole's in sight,
Then you curse the boss for traveling such a doggoned thirsty trail,
You know a hundred better, he's not fit to drive a nail.

Robert W. Gordon Collection
University of Oregon.
Gordon 170: manuscript.

Pariah Canyon, Arizona

Cowboy work is much the same today as it was when the cattle boom first began in the American West in the latter part of the nineteenth century. Though the days of the great trail drives have passed, the industry still thrives on the western ranges, and cowboys are still hired by cattlegrowers to oversee the herds and to perform other necessary jobs.

Cattle are grazed in a rotation system, usually positioned in lower, warmer grounds in winter and moved slowly to the highest ground in summer. Ranch hands are housed in camps, usually in bunk houses or mobile homes. Corrals and working chutes are often situated on theses grounds. Many ranches have both a summer and a winter base camp, and some have smaller, more primitive facilities that are used when the herd is too far from a main camp.

Continued on next page

A cowboy's workload is heaviest during roundup time, which usually takes place once in spring and once in fall. The herd is gathered from the grazing area, driven to working pens, and separated for market. Driving in the herd takes only a day or two on smaller ranches, but can take weeks on larger spreads. Once the cattle are corralled near the working area, calves and adult cows are separated. Steers, heifers and bulls are also separated and most steers are trucked to the nearest market.

Cutting, or separating particular animals from the rest of the group, requires special skills of both the cowboy and the horse. Good cutting horses are known for their intelligence, as well as their quickness and power. Though these horses are incredible athletes, the work is so demanding that they must be replaced with a fresh horse about every forty-five minutes.

Once separated, new calves are driven into special chutes or working pens where they are branded, earmarked, castrated and de-horned – unpleasant, but necessary tasks in the cattle business. Inoculations and other doctoring is also done at roundup time.

Continued on next page

Sawtooth Mountains, Idaho

Cowboys from different outfits in a particular locale often help out during roundups at neighboring ranches – a leftover practice from the days when roundups were massive, joint ventures between outfits. Roundups today are still fast-paced, exhilarating events and are often preceded or followed by a local celebration of some sort. It was from friendly competition between outfits during these rousing events that the sport of rodeo began.

The rest of the year, cowboys oversee the herd, watching for predators, such as wolves, coyotes and mountain lions, making sure there is ample water, and providing medical attention when needed. Cowboys also ride along fenced property, repairing damage to fences and looking for stragglers that need to be returned to the herd. Although most ranches now use pickup trucks or all-terrain vehicles for many jobs, the cowboy will never lose his horse entirely. Some tasks will always be performed best with a well-trained cowpony.

A cowboy's life is still lived on wide-open western ranges. It is hard work for low pay, but few of them would trade it for a more comfortable existence. Some are inexplicably drawn to cowboy work, and it holds a romantic appeal for many of the rest of us. As one Arizona ranch hand said, "We all played 'cowboy' as kids – some of us just never want to quit." ∼

The hills of Virginia city, Montana

Homesickness

The sagebrush ain't a handsome plant –
　　Its color can be beat;
But when you're gone away from it
　　The sage is mighty sweet;
You recollect the wide expanse
　　Of silver-colored plain,
And jest for one more sight of it
　　You'd trade your fields of grain.

The cactus ain't a lovely flower,
　　Competin' with the rose.
But when you're miles and miles away
　　You want it, goodness knows;
You'd wear it, spikes and all, upon
　　The lapel of your vest,
Because it brung to you a hint
Of your brave, open West!

Arthur Chapman
Cactus Center
Houghton Mifflin Co.
Boston, Mass. 1921

Way Out West

When my old soul hunts range and rest
Beyond the last divide,
Just plant me in some stretch of West
That's sunny, lone and wide.
Let cattle rub my tombstone down
And coyotes mourn their kin,
Let hawses paw and tromp the moun'
But don't you fence me in!

Excerpted from:
Badger Clark
Sun and Saddle Leather
Chapman and Grimes
Boston, Mass. 1936

Teton County, Wyoming

Colorado Plateau in Arizona.

Some horses are easier to saddle than others.

The cowboy's distinctive apparel and working gear make him a recognizable figure anywhere. His tall, wide-brimmed hat resembles, perhaps, a kingly crown High-heeled boots and the proud jangle of his spurs help to make him the imposing figure from which his legend was created. Though he may be a laborer, a cowboy mounted on a horse – the most regal of all creatures — looms almost majestically above the rest of humankind.

His throne is a sturdy saddle, developed by the cattle industry specifically for cowboy work. The seat is deep, with a high pommel and cantle. A steel horn, covered with leather, serves as a tethering post for his rope to hold an ornery steer. The fancy engraving found on many cow saddles serves to make them less slippery. The heavy wooden stirrups protect the cowboy's feet from being crushed, and they are often covered with a leather flap to shield his boots from brush.

The rope, or lariat, is an essential tool for cowboy work. Lariats are generally made from three-quarter inch hemp, sometimes thirty feet long, and are stored coiled on the left side of the saddle-horn.

Perhaps the most distinguishing mark of a cowboy is his hat. It has a tall crown and wide brim that is slightly curled on the sides. The shape allows water to run off in back. Most are made of beaver fur and black is the preferred color, although light, straw hats are sometimes worn in hot weather. Hat bands of braided horse hair help to adjust the fit and add a decorative element. The shaping and other features of cowboy hats are guided by regional preferences, and one can often tell where a cowboy is from by looking at his hat.

Continued on next page

Boots are the most costly apparel in a cowboy's wardrobe. They are made of fine leather, with thin soles and pointed or slightly rounded toes for gliding easily into a stirrup. The heels are high, usually one and a half to two and a half inches, providing a secure brace against the stirrup. Boot tops are tall to protect the legs from brush, and many have fancy stitching that provides strength and durability.

Spurs are often attached to cowboy boots help to control a horse. They are attached with leather straps that fit over the insteps and connected to a metal brace that curves around the heel. The rowel, a metal wheel with pointed edges, is attached at the heel. Spurs are used to get a horse's attention, but never to cut or gouge the animal.

Other apparel associated with the cowboy was also designed to be functional. Sturdy, denim jeans, introduced to the laborer in the West by Levi Strauss in the 1850s, are rugged enough to last in rough terrain. Chaps, which are leggings made of leather, cover the outside of the legs to protect them from brush. Vests provide warmth and protection while leaving the arms free, and they also have pockets for storing small items. The colorful bandana associated with the cowboy's attire shields his mouth and nose from dust, serves as a sun shield over his hat, a blinder for his horse, a signal flag and a towel. ~

After the rain, Sonoran Desert, Arizona

Speaking of a Cowboy's Home

Sky is his ceiling, grass is his bed,
saddle is the pillow for the cowboy's head;
Way out West where the antelope roam,
And the coyotes howl 'round the cowboy's home;
Where the miner digs for the golden veins,
Where the prairies are covered with the chapparal frail,
And the valleys are checkered with the cattle trails;
Where the eagles scream and the catamounts squall,
the cowboy's home is the best of all.

From the manuscript
by J.M. Grigsby
Comanche, Tex. 1911

The Philosophical Cowboy

On the Double Circle Range where the grass grows green
The cattle get wild and the broncs get mean,
And the calves get bigger as the days go by,
So we got to keep a-rimming, boys, it's root hog or die.

In the morning after breakfast about daylight
Throw your saddle on a horse and pull your cinches tight,
Your bronc may jump crooked or he may jump high,
But we all got to ride them, boys, it's root hog or die.

Oh the hills are rough and rocky but we got to make the drive,
When you start a bunch of cattle, you better come alive'
If you ever get a maverick you must get him on the fly,
So you better take to them, boys, it's root hog or die.

In the middle of the night it is sometimes awfully hard
To leave your warm blankets when you're called on guard'
And pass the weary moments while the stars are in the sky
Humming to the cattle, boys, it's root hog or die.

Excerpted from the poem by "J.H.S."
(Out West, April 1911, p. 336)

Bringing in supplies, Sierra Nevadas

A Cowboy Lexicon

BED GROUND - (bedding cattle) The place where cattle are gathered to spend the night.

BRAND - (branding, branding iron) An identifying mark, burned into the hide of an animal with a hot iron, to establish ownership. Ranchers register their distinctive brands with local government officials.

BRONC - (bronco, broncho, bronk) A cowhorse in general or a horse that is not broken.

BULL - A male cow that has not been castrated and is able to breed.

CHAPS - Leather coverings worn over pants to protect a rider from rough brush or fences.

CHUCK - (chuck wagon) Food. The outfit's cook transported food and cooking implements in a wagon along the trail or at a roundup.

CHUTE - A narrow passageway, usually built of wooden planks, just wide enough to move livestock from one area to another in single file.

Eating dust.

CORRAL - A fenced-in area where livestock is held, usually temporarily. Can also be a verb.

COW - All individual cattle, regardless of sex, but the term is sometimes used to specify a mature female.

COWBOY - (cowhand, cowman, cowpoke, cowpuncher.) In their broad definitions, these terms can apply to men or women who work cattle as an occupation. The terms hand, poke and puncher can be used without the prefix, cow-.

COWGIRL - Once used to distinguish between male and female cowhands, today the term usually refers to a female who is not a cowboy by profession, but performs in rodeo events.

COWPONY - (pony) A trained ranch horse.

CUT - To separate an animal from the herd. The same verb also means to castrate a steer.

CUTTING HORSE - A very skilled, very athletic horse ridden by a cowboy whose job is to separate individual cows from the herd. The cutting horse is positioned between the selected cow and the other cows to "cut" it from the rest of the herd.

DALLY - As a verb, looping one's rope once around the saddle horn at the instant an animal is caught with the lasso. The noun refers to the loop, which can be released quickly.

DOGIE - a calf, especially one that is separated from its mother.

DRIVE - (cattle drive) As a verb, the process of moving livestock in a group from one location to another. The noun refers to the entire event. Drives from one seasonal grazing area to another often took several weeks on the open range.

DROVER - A cowhand who moves cattle on a drive.

DUDE - Someone from the city visiting a ranch on vacation.

EARMARK - Specific markings, cut on the ears of cows, to separate them into particular classifications, or to distinguish them from cattle belonging to other ranches.

GATE - With the advent of fences separating ranch properties, there is a common code of conduct regarding gates. If you find it open, leave it open. If you find it closed, close it after entering.

GREENHORN - Someone unaccustomed to the difficult conditions or the code of conduct on the range.

HEIFER - A female cow, especially one who has never produced a calf.

LARIAT - (Spanish - la reata) Commonly refers to a rope used to work cattle.

LASSO - A long rope with a running noose at the end. As a verb, to catch with a lasso.

MAVERICK - An unbranded calf of uncertain ownership or a motherless calf.

OUTFIT - All hands working for a particular ranch or on a particular drive. Can also mean an entire ranching operation, including livestock, buildings and equipment.

QUIRT - A leather riding whip, partially braided, with a short stock and long lashes.

REMUDA - A string of horses. Refers to all of the horses belonging to a particular outfit.

REP - A cowboy who represents his brand at a joint roundup. He has an excellent eye, and can spot cattle, marked with his outfit's brand and earmarks, in a vast herd.

RIDING CIRCLE - On a roundup, a certain group of cowboys ride the perimeter of the herd to gather cows that have strayed from the main group. The horses used to ride circle require good stamina.

RIDING FOR THE BRAND - Being loyal to your outfit.

RIDING NIGHT HERD - Riding circle at night around the bedded cattle to prevent them from scattering or stampeding. The horses used to ride night herd require good vision and surefootedness. The cowboys often sing in a soothing tone to calm the cattle.

RIDING THE LINE - Before fences separated ranch properties, the line rider rode the perimeter of his outfit's boundaries to keep strays from joining with another brand's herd.

RODEO - A public exhibition in which the traditional working skills of cowboys are scored in separate events. Calf-roping, steer wrestling, bronc riding and bull riding are some of today's events.

ROUNDUP - An event, usually in the fall and in the spring, where the entire herd is gathered to be counted, worked and separated for sale.

ROWEL - The rotating wheel on a spur.

RUSTLE - To steal cattle. (n. - rustler)

SALOON - An establishment where a cowboy could find beer or whiskey, women and gambling.

SPURS - Metal devices worn around a boot to aid in controlling a horse. The shine and the jingle of the rowels as he walks can make the cowboy an imposing figure.

STAMPEDE - A sudden and frenzied running of the cattle, usually set off by a loud noise. Stampedes are very dangerous for cowboys. Those who fall off of their mounts and are trampled by the cattle, are likely to be seriously injured or killed.

STEER - a male cow that has been castrated.

WORK CATTLE - To work cattle is to perform alterations on cows, especially calves, after they are rounded up. The work includes branding, earmarking, de-horning and castrating.

WRANGLER - A cowboy who takes care of the remuda. ~

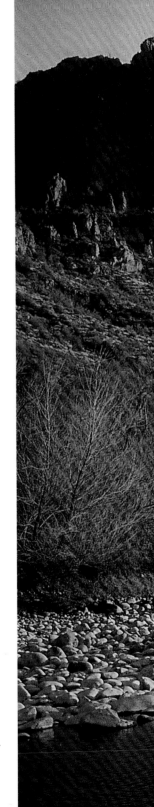

Salt River in southern Arizona.

Who wants to play?

"**If there are not horses in heaven,** I do not want to go there. But I believe there will be . . . . for God loved them or he would not have created them with such majesty . . . . How can I explain to dainty, delicate women what it is like to climb down into a rodeo chute onto the back of a wild horse? . . . . Pain is not too great a price to pay for the freedom of the saddle and a horse between the legs."

—Fanny Sperry Steele,
World Champion
Lady Bucking Horse Rider
1912 and 1913

Fanny Sperry Steele and Helen Clark
"A Horse Beneath Me...Sometimes"
(8,9,12)

Ghost Riders Legend

As a boy, Stan Jones was riding with two old cowhands near Douglas, Arizona. One evening, the sky turned strangely foreboding, as it does before a tornado. The men told young Jones it was an omen in the clouds – a warning for cowboys who are tempted to do wrong. The old legend says there are phantom cowboys in the clouds, chasing the devil's herd across the sky forever as a penance for bad deeds they have done. The tale so impressed Jones that he wrote a song about it, which was later heard by some people from Hollywood. The song, first recorded by Gene Autry in 1949, made the Arizona cowboy successful overnight.

Riders in the Sky – A Cowboy Legend (Verses 3 and 4)

Their faces gaunt, their eyes were blurred and shirts all soaked with sweat —
They're ridin' hard to catch that herd but they ain't caught 'em yet,
'cause they've got to ride forever on that range
up in the sky. On horses snort-in' fire —-
As they ride on, hear their cry:

[Refrain]
Yi-pi-yi-ay, —-
Yi-pi-yi-o, — Ghost riders in — the sky. —-

The rid-ers loped on by him — he
heard one call his name, — "If you want to save
your soul from hell a rid-in' on our range, —-
Then cow-boy change your ways to-day or with
us you will ride — A try'n to catch the
dev-il's herd — A-cross these end-less skies." —

[refrain]

Stan Jones (1914 - 1963)